MW00414867

God's Peace

EXPERIENCE IT ALL THE TIME

LYNETTE HAGIN

18 17 16 15 14 13 12   08 07 06 05 04 03 02

God's Peace: Experience It All the Time
ISBN-13: 978-0-89276-808-0
ISBN-10: 0-89276-808-8

Copyright © 2010 Rhema Bible Church
aka Kenneth Hagin Ministries, Inc.
All rights reserved.
Printed in USA

In the U.S. write:
Kenneth Hagin Ministries
P.O. Box 50126
Tulsa, OK 74150-0126
1-888-28-FAITH
www.rhema.org

In Canada write:
Kenneth Hagin Ministries of Canada
P.O. Box 335, Station D
Etobicoke (Toronto), Ontario
Canada M9A 4X3
1-866-70-RHEMA
www.rhemacanada.org

Table of Contents

Introduction

Are the cares of life threatening to overtake you? Do you wrestle with fear and anxiety or have trouble getting a good night's sleep?

Or perhaps there's a cloud of worries that seems to be hanging over you. Maybe you've been tormented by terrible memories—mental pictures that keep coming back to haunt your mind.

When turmoil and distress try to come upon me, the only true peace I have found has come from the Word of God. Psalm 119:105 tells us, *"Thy word is a lamp unto my feet, and a light unto my path."* Just as a candle provides light in a darkened room, God's Word brings light, encouragement, and peace to any situation.

As you read this book, allow the living Word of God to be a light to your path. Call upon Jesus—the Prince of Peace—and cast your cares on Him. He will sustain you in the dark times, the times of trouble. He will give you peace in place of confusion and unsettledness.

As Numbers 6:26 (Amplified) tells us, He will give us "tranquility of heart and life continually!" That's what

1

God wants for you—a life of peace, a life of fulfillment, and a life of tranquility. So allow the peace of God to rule in your heart and embrace His peace for your life today!

CHAPTER 1

The Lord Our Peace

"Peace I leave with you, my peace I give unto you: not as the world giveth, give I unto you. Let not your heart be troubled, neither let it be afraid."
—John 14:27

Peace, wonderful peace! The Lord has said that He would give us peace. And not just any kind of peace— His peace. That thought has been rumbling over and over in my spirit lately.

In the world we live in, we desperately need peace. The turmoil around us is mind-boggling. Reports of wars, earthquakes, floods, and every other type of calamity fill the news. Crime is prevalent all over the world. It seems that the only thing we read about in the newspaper is tragedies.

Meanwhile, man has more conveniences and luxuries than ever before, and many of them are designed to save time as well as make our lives easier. All we have to

3

do is push a button here and push a button there and things get done!

With all of our modern conveniences, you would think that we would have *more* time on our hands. But I have found the exact opposite to be true. Despite modern technology, we seem to have less time. And in spite of having every convenience possible, there is no peace.

Thank God, our Heavenly Father has made a provision for us to have peace! Romans 5:1 says, *"Therefore being justified by faith, we have peace with God through our Lord Jesus Christ."*

God loved us so much that He sent His one and only Son, Jesus Christ, to redeem mankind and restore our peace with Him. According to John 10:10, Jesus came that we might have life and have it more abundantly—a life that's filled with God's blessings and His *peace*.

Of course, we cannot have peace without knowing the Prince of Peace. We must accept Jesus Christ as our Lord and Savior before we can experience true peace.

Sadly, there are many people today who have accepted Jesus Christ as their Lord and Savior and yet they still have no peace. Why? Because they have not accepted the Lord as their Peace Giver. He is not only our Savior, but He is also our Peace Giver.

When we look to Jesus as our Peace Giver, He can help us cope with everyday life, and He can do it without the aid of addictive chemicals. He is the Problem Solver, not the problem maker.

I know when things begin to crumble under my feet—and they do crumble sometimes—Jesus is the One I turn to. You see, just because we become a Christian doesn't mean that everything is going to be a bed of roses. We're still going to go through trials and struggles. We're still going to experience problems. In fact, Jesus Himself told us that in this world we're going to have tribulation.

In John 16:33, the Lord said, *"These things I have spoken unto you, that in me ye might have peace. In the world ye shall have tribulation: but be of good cheer; I have overcome the world."* Jesus is telling us that we may go through problems. We may go through rough places and deep valleys, but we're not going to camp in those valleys. We're going to walk through them *in peace* knowing that our Lord Jesus Christ has overcome the world.

Instead of turning to the Lord for peace, many people today—including some Christians—are turning to drugs and alcohol to help them find peace. But God can carry us through the dark days and troubled times without altering our body chemistry!

Besides, drugs and alcohol can only give us temporary peace. But my God can give us permanent peace. In times of anxiety and stress, we must turn to the Lord because He is our peace! And He's the only One Who can lead us safely through the storms of life!

5

Jesus Covered It All

What is peace? Webster's Dictionary defines peace as "freedom from disquieting or oppressive thoughts or emotions."[1] The Hebrew word for peace is *shalom*, and it indicates the idea of soundness of health—physically, mentally, emotionally, and spiritually.[2] God's peace covers it all!

When the crisis times come, it's important for us to know what our Heavenly Father has provided for us in His Word. Isaiah 53 tells us that Jesus not only died for our salvation and bore our sicknesses, but He also bore our griefs and carried our sorrows. He bore our emotional problems, weaknesses, and distresses. Let's read those verses from *The Amplified Bible*.

ISAIAH 53:4–5 (Amplified)

4 Surely He has borne our griefs (sicknesses, weaknesses, and distresses) and carried our sorrows and pains [of punishment], yet we [ignorantly] considered Him stricken, smitten, and afflicted by God [as if with leprosy].

5 But He was wounded for our transgressions, He was bruised for our guilt and iniquities; the chastisement [needful to obtain] peace and well-being for us was upon Him, and with the stripes [that wounded] Him we are healed and made whole.

Verse 5 says that Jesus Christ bore "the chastisement needful to obtain our peace and well-being." He bore it for us! We need to take God literally at His Word and receive the peace that He has already provided for us!

So often, we grab hold of the promise in this scripture of healing for our physical bodies, but we forget that God has also promised us emotional and mental healing. As a result, we don't call upon the Lord to help us with problems in those areas. But we can be healed in *every* area of our lives and experience God's wonderful peace all the time!

A Solid Foundation That Never Shakes

How do we receive this peace that only God can give? Let's look at Isaiah chapter 26, first in the *King James Version* and then in *The Amplified Bible.*

ISAIAH 26:3–4

3 Thou wilt keep him in perfect peace, whose mind is stayed on thee: because he trusteth in thee.

4 Trust ye in the Lord for ever: for in the Lord Jehovah is everlasting strength.

ISAIAH 26:3–4 (Amplified)

3 You will guard him and keep him in perfect and constant peace whose mind [both its inclination and its character] is stayed on You, because HE COMMITS HIMSELF TO YOU, leans on You, and hopes confidently in You.

4 So trust in the Lord (COMMIT YOURSELF TO HIM, lean on Him, hope confidently in Him) forever; for the Lord God is an everlasting Rock [the Rock of Ages].

Let me ask you today: Have you truly committed yourself to the Lord? Do you continually lean on Him? I lean on my Heavenly Father on a daily basis. If we want to have peace, we must commit our ways to the Lord and lean on Him continually.

Psalm 37:5 says, *"Commit thy way unto the Lord; trust also in him; and he shall bring it to pass."* So many times we wonder why we don't have peace, but we are not committing all of our ways unto the Lord. In some areas we are; in others we are not. But if we're going to live peaceful lives, we must commit our entire being to Him.

Notice verse 4 of Isaiah 26 (Amplified). It says, *". . . for the Lord God is an everlasting Rock [the Rock of Ages]."* I can tell you from my own experience that you can stand confidently on that "Everlasting Rock," because He will never shake. He will never crumble. That Rock won't even tremble. Even if the whole world around you is shaking, you can hold steady on your Rock—the Lord Jesus Christ!

I have never experienced an earthquake, but several years ago my husband, Ken, and I were in Peru, and we experienced some tremors. We were in our hotel room at the time, which was located on the 10th floor. We were already in bed, just about to drift off to sleep, when the room suddenly started shaking. I had no idea what was happening, so I said to my husband, "Honey, what is that?"

"It's tremors," he replied. I knew Ken had experienced tremors when he was stationed in Taiwan in the army. I didn't realize how severe these tremors were until all of a sudden I heard him take authority over them, saying, "In the Name of Jesus!" I knew the situation must be serious if he was calling on the Name of Jesus for our safety and protection. We later learned that those tremors were about a five on the Richter scale.

It was extremely frightening when the earth around me was trembling. But as believers, we always have a solid foundation to stand on. We can plant our feet firmly on our Rock, and we can have peace even when the world around us trembles!

Draw Close to Him

Let's read Isaiah 26:3 again: *"Thou wilt keep him in perfect peace, whose mind is stayed on thee: because he trusteth in thee."* The problem with most of us is that we're trying to live a peaceful and victorious life without keeping our minds on the Lord Jesus Christ.

Have you ever noticed how, when life is going smoothly, we sometimes forget about keeping our minds on the Lord? When everything seems to be so wonderful, we find ourselves drifting away from God and neglecting our relationship with Him. In some cases, we may even start relying on our own abilities instead of leaning on the Lord. But as soon as trouble strikes, we go rushing back to the Father. Thankfully, He's always there for us!

9

It's the same way with us as earthly parents. As our children grow older, they sometimes drift away from us. But the instant they get into trouble or find themselves in rough waters, what do they do? They cry out to Mom and Dad for help!

If we're going to live the peaceful life that God desires for us to live, our relationship with the Lord must be continually growing stronger, not diminishing. We must constantly draw close to Him and rely on Him instead of putting our trust and confidence in our own abilities. Our strength comes from the Lord Jesus Christ. It's only *in Him* that we can do all things (Phil. 4:13)!

I'll never forget how the crowds flocked to church after the 9-11 terrorist attack on America. All of a sudden, people decided to draw close to the Lord because they had experienced a horrible disaster.

I was thrilled for all the people who came to church during that time, but my heart hurt that they hadn't been there *every* Sunday to draw close to the Lord. I'll tell you, it's more important than ever for us to *stay* close to our Heavenly Father—so close that He is guiding our every step!

I am always amazed when I hear people give their testimonies, and they say, "I'm so thankful for this trial or this awful thing that's happened because it brought me closer to the Lord."

No! We do not have to wait until we're driven to our knees by a crisis to draw close to God. We have the privilege of communing with our Heavenly Father on a daily basis.

Serving God should be a way of life, not just a Sunday experience. Serving the Lord has always been my way of life. My parents were pastors, and they taught me to make God the center of my life. I am so thankful for the close relationship I have with the Lord today—He's my Best Friend!

Unfortunately, God is often *not* at the center of people's lives today—even for Christians. It seems that we're rushing from one ball game or sports event to another, from this activity to that, while church takes second place for us. And that grieves my heart! I believe this is one of the reasons why we don't have any peace!

We need to get back to the place where our Heavenly Father is at the center of our lives and everything revolves around Him. We need to commune with the Lord, keep His Word in our hearts, and stay close to Him at all times. When we give the Lord first place and continually stir up our hunger for the things of God, we will find our total peace in Him!

Keep Your Mind on the Mountain Mover

As long as we're living on this earth, we're going to encounter distressing situations. We're going to experience times of pressure. There will always be challenges—mountains to climb and valleys to dig our way out of. But we can still have peace.

Sometimes we get so involved in thinking about our mountain of problems that we forget to keep our minds on the Mountain Mover. When we keep our minds on our Heavenly Father, we're not going to worry about the troubles in the economy. We're not going to worry about the stock market—is it going up or is it going down? Everything around us may be spinning, but our confidence will be in God and His Word!

There's an old song that says, "I trust in God wherever I may be, Upon the land or on the rolling sea, For, come what may, from day to day, My heav'nly Father watches over me."[3]

God is watching over us! And His desire is that we live a life of peace, a life of joy, and a life of abundance. As we keep our minds focused on the Lord and lean on Him, the struggles will fade away, the turmoil will cease, and He will give us a peace that nothing else can!

CHAPTER 2

What Are You Thinking?

"And the peace of God, which passeth all understanding, shall keep your hearts and minds through Christ Jesus."
—Philippians 4:7

The mind can be a powerful ally or an awesome enemy. The trouble so many of us experience in life is in our minds—we let our thoughts run wild! If we want to live peaceful lives, we must guard our minds and control our thought lives. *We* must do something about it!

Of course, we live in a negative society. If it's not bad news, it's usually not considered newsworthy. If you listen to the news reports for very long, you might not even want to get out of your house!

Even in the Christian world, so many times all we hear is bad news. We hear the latest gossip or people rush to tell us reports of trouble and strife.

Meanwhile, Satan is playing havoc with our minds. He constantly bombards us with negative thoughts. He brings all kinds of imaginations to our minds, trying to fill us with anxiety so he can keep us from having the peace we can experience with God.

Did you know that the enemy is out to destroy us? First Peter 5:8 says, *"Be sober, be vigilant; because your adversary the devil, as a roaring lion, walketh about, seeking whom he may devour."* Notice this verse says, *". . . seeking whom he MAY devour."* It doesn't say that the devil is going to devour us. It says that is he is looking for people who will *allow him* to devour them.

How does Satan devour people? First of all, he specializes in fear. He tries to torment us with fearful, worrisome thoughts. The devil, unlike the Holy Spirit, is not a gentleman. If we open the door to Satan even a tiny crack, he'll kick it wide open!

That's why the Bible says, *"Neither give place to the devil"* (Eph. 4:27). We cannot allow the enemy to dominate our thought lives no matter how hard he tries. He will try to dog our tracks, but if we give in and begin to meditate on those negative thoughts we'll be defeated. Fear is a spirit and it will get a grip on us if we allow it to.

Thank goodness, we don't have to fear. We don't have to worry. We don't have to let our minds be cluttered with troublesome thoughts. If we will keep our thoughts focused on the right things, our Heavenly Father will deliver us and keep us in perfect peace.

Thoughts May Come but Thoughts Must Go!

In Philippians chapter 4, the Apostle Paul tells us how to deal with worrisome thoughts.

PHILIPPIANS 4:6–7

6 Be careful for nothing; but in every thing by prayer and supplication with thanksgiving let your requests be made known unto God.

7 And the peace of God, which passeth all under-standing, shall keep your hearts and minds through Christ Jesus.

PHILIPPIANS 4:6–7 (Amplified)

6 Do not fret or have any anxiety about anything, but in every circumstance and in everything, by prayer and petition (definite requests), with thanksgiving, con-tinue to make your wants known to God.

7 And God's peace [shall be yours, that tranquil state of a soul assured of its salvation through Christ, and so fearing nothing from God and being content with its earthly lot of whatever sort that is, that peace] which transcends all understanding shall garrison and mount guard over your hearts and minds in Christ Jesus.

God is saying in these verses that He doesn't want us to have any worries or anxious thoughts about our needs. When a problem strikes, instead of panicking, He wants us to pray—to make our requests known to Him. We can say to Him, "Father, this is what I need," and He will be right there to help us!

Do you know how much God cares for you? He is concerned about whatever you are concerned about. According to James 4:2, we have not because we ask not. If we will ask the Lord for the things we need in faith, according to God's Word, there's nothing our Father won't give us. He loves to accommodate His children!

Naturally speaking, don't most parents love to give things to their children? The Word says, *"If ye . . . know how to give good gifts unto your children, how much more shall your Father which is in heaven give good things to them that ask him?"* (Matt. 7:11). Our Heavenly Father loves us so much more than we can imagine, and He is willing to give us whatever we need, if we will just ask!

I don't know about you, but if I'm troubled about something or if depression tries to overtake me, I feel so much better after I've prayed. I feel stronger and I have so much more peace. Why? When I make my requests known to my Heavenly Father, I am able to draw on His strength. And in His strength, I can do all things (Phil. 4:13)— including guard my mind from negative thoughts!

Think on These Things

After Paul tells us to "be careful for nothing," but to make our requests known to the Lord, he gives us specific instructions about what God wants us to think about.

PHILIPPIANS 4:8

8   Finally, brethren, whatsoever things are true, whatsoever things are honest, whatsoever things are just,

whatsoever things are pure, whatsoever things are lovely, whatsoever things are of good report; if there be any virtue, and if there be any praise, think on these things.

Of course, things aren't always lovely. Things aren't always true, honest, or of a good report. But Paul is saying here, "Don't focus on the negative things. Think about the things that will build you up and not tear you down. Think about all the good things God has done for you—all the promises He's given you in His Word. Focus on the positive things in life."

Are those the things that are consuming your thoughts today—the good things of God? Or are you thinking about the difficulties that lie ahead of you, the challenges and obstacles that are blocking your path? Are you finding fault with everything and everybody around you? Are you always focusing on the things that have gone wrong?

Some people constantly dwell on their own faults and weaknesses. They think about all the mistakes they've made in the past. They always ponder the "what-ifs" of life.

When we think about those things, we're focusing on the wrong reality. Those kinds of thoughts are going to get us into trouble, and they will also rob us of our peace!

Let's read what David had to say about the thoughts that sometimes plagued his mind:

PSALM 55:1–2 (NIV)

1   Listen to my prayer, O God, do not ignore my plea;

2   hear me and answer me. My thoughts trouble me and I am distraught.

David said, "My thoughts trouble me and I am distraught." His were disturbing him. They were making him anxious and uneasy. If we're not careful, the same thing will happen to us.

It's so important for us to stop thinking the wrong kinds of thoughts. We need to stop telling ourselves, "This project is never going to get off the ground. I'm never going to get ahead. I'm bound to lose. My life will always be out of control."

You cannot think thoughts of defeat and expect victory. You cannot think thoughts of weakness and expect strength. And you cannot think thoughts of confusion and fear and expect peace!

What are some of the thoughts we should be thinking?

HEBREWS 12:2–3

2   Looking unto Jesus the author and finisher of our faith; who for the joy that was set before him endured the cross, despising the shame, and is set down at the right hand of the throne of God.

3   For consider him that endured such contradiction of sinners against himself, lest ye be wearied and faint in your minds.

18

When the enemy tries to fill our minds with distressing thoughts, these verses encourage us to look to Jesus and think about how much He loves us and what He endured for us—the shame of the Cross. When we focus on these things, we will not grow weary and faint in our minds.

Besides, if we're meditating on God's promises and thinking about the good things of God, we won't have time to worry and complain or get discouraged and depressed. We will always be filled with a good report— the report of God's Word.

What does God's report say? His report says, "All things are working together for my good" (Rom. 8:28). His report says, "Nothing can separate me from the love of Christ" (Rom. 8:35–39). His report says, "I can do all things through Christ Who strengthens me" (Phil. 4:13)!

His report also says—and these words are found throughout the Bible—"It shall come to pass." Now think about that for a moment. This trouble, this trial, this problem you've been struggling with, hasn't come to *stay*. It's come to *pass*—because we always triumph in Christ (2 Cor. 2:14)!

Guard Your Mind

We're all human. We all have trouble with our minds. We all struggle with our thoughts and emotions. Yes, we're standing on the Word. We're making our faith

19

confessions. But all kinds of thoughts are still whirling through our minds!

Sometimes we're like David was in those verses we just read from the Book of Psalms. Our thoughts trouble us, we wrestle with terrible fears, and worry is dogging our tracks.

You may be so burdened in your spirit right now until there's no joy left in your heart. It's important not to allow those anxious, fearful thoughts to reign in your life. Instead, I encourage you to guard your mind and put your trust in the Lord. As you do, He will give you peace—that perfect peace which passes all understanding!

When you live the kind of life where your thoughts are constantly focused on God and His Word, you won't have any more down days. You won't have any more blue days. You won't be down in the mulligrubs. You won't have to wonder, *What am I going to do next?* And you won't have to live without peace.

Every time you're troubled with distressing thoughts, don't wrestle with them in the mental realm. Just begin to draw upon the Word of God on the inside of you, and keep your thoughts focused on what God says. You'll be surprised at how quickly you'll be surrounded with His presence, and your heart and mind will be filled with His wonderful peace!

CHAPTER 3

Just Trust!

*"Trust in the Lord with all thine heart; and
lean not unto thine own understanding. In all
thy ways acknowledge him, and he shall
direct thy paths."*
—Proverbs 3:5–6

How do we trust in the Lord with all of our hearts?
How do we lean on the everlasting arms of God?

Proverbs 3 tells us first of all that we must *not* lean
to our own understanding, but lean on the understanding of the Lord. We must *not* try to figure things out in
our natural minds—we'll only get things muddled! It's
not our understanding, but His understanding that we
rely on. It's not our wisdom, but His wisdom.

It seems, as human beings, that we want to put our
trust in everything besides the Lord. When we're struggling with the cares and worries of life, we try to rely on
anything we can think of until there's nothing left to rely
on but the Lord Jesus Christ.

21

How many times have we said, "I did everything I knew to do and finally I had to pray"? If we would pray first, if we would turn to the Lord first, frustration would leave us. Depression would leave us. Distress and discouragement would fly away!

Of course, it's impossible for us to have peace if we don't trust in the Lord. We must develop such a trust in our Heavenly Father and lean on His arms to such an extent that we know He's always there for us and we never doubt the promises of God.

The disciples had to learn to trust in the Lord—to trust in His Word. In Mark chapter 4, they climbed into a boat with Jesus, and He said to them, *"Let us pass over unto the other side"* (v. 35). Now Jesus wasn't concerned about making it to the other side of the lake because He had spoken the words, "Let us pass over to the other side." So what did He do? He lay down in the boat and went to sleep!

Guess what happened? A storm suddenly erupted, and the disciples panicked. They awakened Jesus and began to cry out, "Master, don't You even care that we perish?" (v. 38).

And isn't that what happens to us sometimes? Jesus has told us, "Take hold of My hand and we're going to pass over to the other side of this problem." At first, we're so happy because Jesus has said that we're going to the other side. But all of a sudden, the boat starts rocking, the waves start rising, and we're gripped with fear. That's exactly what happened to the disciples!

I'm sure Jesus was probably thinking, *Didn't I tell you that we were going to the other side?* And He actually did rebuke the disciples when He said, "Oh ye of little faith. Why are you so afraid?" (v. 40). But He still said to the storm, *"Peace, be still"* (v. 39), and the waves grew calm. And He and the disciples crossed over to the other side.

The Lord is saying to you and me today, "Didn't I tell you that we're going to the other side? Look to Me. Put your trust in Me." When we get into the boat of life with the Lord Jesus Christ, even if the waters get rough and stormy, we can rest with assurance that we're going to the other side!

Rather than trust in the Lord, many times we're like the disciples. We get our eyes on the situation instead of on the One Who is the Master over every situation. We panic, and we think we're not going to make it. We're stressed out, worn out, and not effective for God because we're worrying so desperately about making it to the other side!

Or we decide to go to the other side by our own route. We want to go in our own timing. But God's route is not always our route, and His timing is not always our timing. It doesn't matter what route or timing God chooses, His promises are always true and what He said He would do, He will do. Just trust Him! Trust Him! Trust in the Lord!

Stay Out of the Arena of Questioning God

Discouraging times come to all of us. I understand how exasperating the circumstances of life can be. I understand the dilemmas that can plague our minds. But the most important thing I ever had to determine in my life was to trust in the Lord with all of my heart and not get into the arena of questioning God.

There have been times when I have wanted to say, "Why, Lord? Why is this happening to me?" Oh, I have wanted to question Him so many times! And the enemy is always tugging at our coattails, trying to cause us to question the Lord.

My father-in-law, the late Kenneth E. Hagin, always encouraged us to trust in the Lord and not get into the arena of questioning. As believers, one of the most important things that we must do is not waver (James 1:6). We cannot question "why, why, why?" Those questions are a roadblock, and they can hinder our relationship with our Heavenly Father.

During times when I've struggled with questions and doubts, I finally had to rest in the fact that God is God. I had to decide that my confidence is in the Word and that God is bound to perform what He has promised in His Word.

I told the Lord, "I'm not going to question You. I'm not even going to take up my time asking those kinds of questions. There are more important things I need to hear from You rather than questioning why something has already happened the way it has."

Sometimes I've literally had to play one particular song by David Ingles over and over again to bring peace to my mind. It says, "My confidence is great in the Lord, Because I believe in God's Word."[1] I had to repeat it and repeat it until I finally believed it. We may need to hear things over and over before they sink in. Why? Because our heads get in the way. It's so easy for us to get trapped in the mental arena!

When we're tempted to question the Lord, we need to recognize that we don't have all the answers to the situations we face in life. We may not know why our loved one passed away or why we've been struck by some terrible sickness. We may not understand why we're being battered by the devil's attack. But we have to get past all of those questions.

Ultimately, we have to focus on the things that we *do know*. We do know that we serve a good God, a God Who loves us and is able to do exceedingly and abundantly above all that we could ever ask or think (Eph. 3:20). We do know that in all of these things we are more than conquerors through Jesus Christ (Rom. 8:37). We do know that Jesus bore our sins and sicknesses on the cross and by His stripes we are healed (1 Pet. 2:24). If we focus on the truth of God's Word, it will hold us steady, even when the questions are swirling through our minds.

Often, we continue to ask God questions when all He wants us to do is grab hold of His hand and say, "God, we're in this together. Let's go to the other side!" We will never be happy or have any peace in our hearts until we trust the Lord with our entire being.

I love to read Proverbs 3:5–6 in *The Message* Bible because it gets right to the point!

PROVERBS 3:5–6 (Message)

5 Trust God from the bottom of your heart; don't try to figure out everything on your own.

6 Listen for God's voice in everything you do, everywhere you go; he's the one who will keep you on track.

God is the One Who will keep us on track. But He can only keep us on track *when we trust in Him*. Trust! The word *trust* means "to place confidence in; rely on; to commit or place in one's care or keeping; entrust.[2]

I believe we are at a place now, with the turmoil we've seen in the economy over the past few years, where we *have* to put our trust in the Lord. We *have* to put our entire confidence in what He said in His Word.

Sometimes that's difficult to do when so many people are struggling. Some have lost their jobs while others have suffered serious financial setbacks. It seems that the attacks have been more horrendous than ever— even against Christians. We're trying desperately to not be moved by what we see, even though things don't always appear to be getting better.

We cannot put our confidence in what the economic forecast says. We must put our trust in what God says. We have to stay with the truth of God's Word. We must take our authority in Christ, make our requests known to Him, and trust in the Lord. It takes doing all of these things—praying, taking our authority, speaking the Word, and trusting God—to get us safely through the storms of life!

There's a song Andraé Crouch wrote many years ago that urges us to put our trust in God's Word, no matter what. It says, "I've had many tears and sorrows; I've had questions for tomorrow. . . ." But the chorus continues, "Through it all, through it all, Oh I've learned to trust in Jesus, I've learned to trust in God. Through it all, through it all, Oh I've learned to depend upon His Word."[3]

What would we do without the Word of God? What would we do without His promises? That's what gets us through the rough waters. That's what gets us through the fiery trials of life—knowing that our God will never fail us, and depending on His Word.

We went through an era in the '70s, '80s, and even the '90s, when we concentrated on learning the Word of God—what our rights are in Christ, the authority of the believer, and how to build our faith. We exercised what we had learned, and the blessings of God came. But in some cases, we became so engrossed with the way God was blessing us that we forgot to continually exercise our faith and trust in God.

I believe we are at the place now where we must revive that which is on the inside of us and exercise strong faith again. It doesn't matter if there's doom and gloom in the economic forecast. It doesn't matter if the boat of our life is rocking and reeling. Our God is able and willing to take care of His own!

Who Do You Trust?

In the natural, we easily place our trust and confidence in other people. For example, let's say that our boss tells us we're going to get a raise. Before payday arrives—before we even see that money—we go out and spend it. Why? Because we trust that what our boss said was true.

Let me give you another example. When our grandchildren were young, they would stand on the edge of the platform at church and jump into my husband's— their Poppy's—arms. They trusted that when they jumped, Poppy was going to catch them. They had complete confidence in their Poppy because he had never missed.

I remember one particular time when our oldest grandson, Cameron, got really bold. Poppy was close to the platform, but he had his back turned and was talking to someone else. All of a sudden, Cameron leaped off the platform and hollered, "Poppy!" in mid-air. My husband had to whirl around and grab him so he wouldn't fall and hurt himself.

That incident gave Ken quite a scare, but he was thankful that he had been close by and had reacted quickly enough to catch Cameron. He told him, "Don't do that again until you get Poppy's attention!"

Thank goodness, we don't have to forewarn our Heavenly Father when we need Him. We always have his attention! And He's much more capable of catching us than anyone in the natural.

Of course, children trust so easily. Just as our grandsons placed their trust in their "Poppy," God desires for us to place our complete trust in Him. And we don't have to worry about the Lord dropping us. He's going to carry us safely through the problems and struggles of life!

Skiing Blind

I have a powerful story to share with you about a group of blind skiers who learned what it means to trust someone completely. It reads:

> "A television program preceding the 1988 Winter Olympics featured blind skiers being trained for slalom skiing, impossible as that sounds. Paired with sighted skiers, the blind skiers were taught on the flats how to make right and left turns. When that was mastered, they were taken to the slalom slope where their sighted partners skied beside them, shouting 'Left!' and 'Right!' As they obeyed the commands, they

were able to negotiate the course and cross the finish line, depending solely on the sighted skier's word. It was either complete trust or catastrophe."[4]

Those blind skiers trusted their partners so much that when they shouted, "left," they turned left. When they shouted, "right," they turned right. And with their partners' help, they skied all the way down the slope. They crossed the finish line because they depended solely on the sighted skiers' words.

That's how we need to be with the Lord. When He tells us to turn left, we need to turn left. When He tells us to turn right, we need to instantly obey His voice. It sounds so simple. But my, how many times do we have to learn that lesson? It seems that we have to learn it over and over again. But if we want to walk in God's peace, we need to rely solely on Him.

Trust and Praise

I don't know of anyone in the Bible who trusted his God more than David did. But in spite of his deep trust in the Lord, I'm sure he must have had trouble with his mind just as we do. I believe that's why he wrote so many times in the Book of Psalms about trusting in God.

PSALM 18:2–3

2   The Lord is my rock, and my fortress, and my deliverer; my God, my strength, in whom I will trust; my

buckler, and the horn of my salvation, and my high tower.

3   I will call upon the Lord, who is worthy to be praised: so shall I be saved from mine enemies.

David said, "I will call upon the Lord"—Who is what? "Who is worthy to be praised." David knew how to praise his God. And we need to learn how to praise our God—our Healer, our Provider, our Strengthener, and the One Who gives us peace.

PSALM 56:3–4

3   What time I am afraid, I will trust in thee.

4   In God I will praise his word, in God I have put my trust; I will not fear what flesh can do unto me.

When fear tries to grip you, what does this psalm say to do? Trust in the Lord. Then it says, "In God I will praise his word." David is saying, "Trust and praise."

PSALM 56:9

9   When I cry unto thee, then shall mine enemies turn back: this I know; for God is for me.

Always remember that your God is for you. The Lord Most High, the Creator of the universe, is on your side! You don't have to be afraid. All you have to do is trust!

PSALM 56:11–12

11   In God have I put my trust: I will not be afraid what man can do unto me.

31

> *12* Thy vows are upon me, O God: I will render praises
> unto thee.

David said, "I will render praises unto thee." When our backs are against the wall, when there's pain racking our bodies, what do we do? We lift our hands and give the Lord praise. When the bills are piling up, when the symptoms have struck and we're tempted to fear, what do we do? We trust and praise our God!

Praise Him for what He has done. Praise Him for what He is going to do. Praise Him for His mighty works! The Lord inhabits the praises of His people (Ps. 22:3)!

There are some who have marveled when my husband and I have gone through difficult or distressing times, and they've asked us, "How have you made it?" We've made it the same way David did, the same way Abraham did, and the same way the older saints did. We've lifted our hands and given praise to the Lord. We've trusted and praised our God!

' 'Tis So Sweet to Trust in Jesus'

Have you come to the place in your walk with the Lord where you trust in Him with all of your heart and you're not leaning on your own understanding? Have you come to the place where you're acknowledging God in all of your ways?

You may have had a terrible time with the circumstances in your past. You may be struggling with questions that are tormenting your mind. Perhaps you've asked the Lord, "Why God? Why did this happen to me? I've stood on Your Word, I've prayed, and I've tried to be obedient to You." If you want to have peace in your heart, you have to stop questioning the Lord. Remember, He is big enough to bring you through *every* situation in victory.

You may be concentrating so hard on what has happened in the past that you can't move on to what God has for you right now. Don't dwell on the past. Just fix your eyes on the goal that God has set before you, and as Paul said in Philippians 3:14, *press on!*

I encourage you today to look ahead—reach toward the future—and put your trust in the Lord! There's an old song we used to sing that says, " *'Tis so sweet to trust in Jesus, Just to take Him at His Word; Just to rest upon His promise; Just to know, 'Thus saith the Lord.' Jesus, Jesus, how I trust Him, How I've prov'd Him o'er and o'er. Jesus, Jesus, Precious Jesus! O for grace to trust Him more."* [5]

It doesn't matter how big your problems are. It doesn't matter how difficult the path you've been traveling. No matter how much the enemy threatens you, you can trust God to take care of it all! He is greater than any test or trial. He is greater than any obstacle. Our Heavenly Father is greater than *all!*

CHAPTER 4

Call Upon the Lord

*"The righteous cry out, and the
Lord hears, And delivers them
out of all their troubles."*
—Psalm 34:17 (NKJV)

It's so wonderful to be able to call upon the Lord in prayer! It's so great to be able to come boldly into His presence! There's nothing like being in the Presence of the Lord—praising Him, worshipping Him, and seeking His face. Sometimes we don't know how desperately we need God's peace until we get into His presence!

When we say, "Heavenly Father, I just want to come into the throne room and fellowship with You," it floods our hearts with peace. There is so much our Heavenly Father wants to tell us, but we have to take the time to commune with Him. And the more we commune with Him, the more we will experience His peace.

There's a verse from the Book of Psalms that was quickened to me when I began to think about seeking the Lord in prayer.

PSALM 34:10

> *10* The young lions do lack, and suffer hunger: but they
> that seek the Lord shall not want any good thing.

Are you "wanting" or lacking some good things in
your life? Are you lacking peace? If you are, let me ask
you this question: have you been seeking the Lord?

Notice verse 15 in this same chapter from the Book
of Psalms.

> *15* The eyes of the Lord are upon the righteous, and his
> ears are open unto their cry.

I'm so thankful that the eyes of the Lord are upon us
and His ears are open to our cries! But what do we have
to do in order for His ears to be open to our cries? Let's
look at verses 13 and 14.

> *13* Keep thy tongue from evil, and thy lips from speaking
> guile.
> *14* Depart from evil, and do good; seek peace, and pur-
> sue it.

If we want God to hear and answer our prayers, if
we want to have His peace in our hearts, we must keep
our lips from guile. It's so important to keep our lips
from saying the wrong things—from saying hurtful
words and spreading gossip.

Verse 17 goes on to say:

> *17* The righteous cry, and the Lord heareth, and deliv-
> ereth them out of all their troubles.

Troubles may come to all of us, but what does this verse say? The Lord hears our cry and He delivers us. Out of *some* of our troubles? No! He delivers us out of them *all*!

You might say, "But I've been living right. I've kept my lips from speaking guile. But when I've cried out to the Lord, He doesn't seem to hear me."

Or you may be thinking, *So-and-so isn't living right, but everything they pray about comes to pass. What's wrong, Lord?*

God doesn't mind if we express our true feelings to Him. He doesn't get upset if we ask Him questions. There's a big difference between asking God our honest questions and getting into the arena of questioning the Lord. Psalm chapter 37 tells us what to do when we have those kinds of questions.

PSALM 37:7–9

7 Rest in the Lord, and wait patiently for him: fret not thyself because of him who prospereth in his way, because of the man who bringeth wicked devices to pass.

8 Cease from anger, and forsake wrath: fret not thyself in any wise to do evil.

9 For evildoers shall be cut off: but those that wait upon the Lord, they shall inherit the earth.

If you have been praying diligently and earnestly about something, and yet the answers haven't come, I believe the Lord is saying to you through these verses, "Rest in Me and I will bring it to pass."

In other words, don't worry or fret about that situation any longer. Just rest in Him. Hebrews 4:3 says, *"We which have believed do enter into REST."* When we rest, we're at peace, aren't we?

Let's look at a few more verses from Hebrews chapter 4.

HEBREWS 4:14–16

14 Seeing then that we have a great high priest, that is passed into the heavens, Jesus the Son of God, let us hold fast our profession.

15 For we have not an high priest which cannot be touched with the feeling of our infirmities; [Jesus knows how we feel!] but was in all points tempted like as we are, yet without sin.

Verse 16 is the verse I want to emphasize here.

16 Let us therefore come boldly unto the throne of grace, that we may obtain mercy, and find grace to help in time of need.

We can come boldly to the Throne of God, and as we do, our Father is going to hear our prayers and He is going to answer us. Hebrews 13:6 says, *"We may boldly say, The Lord is my helper, and I will not fear what man shall do unto me."* *The Message* Bible puts it this way, *"God is there, ready to help; I'm fearless no matter what. Who or what can get to me?"*

God is our Helper. All we have to do is call upon Him and He promises to be there to help us—to answer each and every need.

The more you call upon the Lord in prayer, the more you will walk in His peace, knowing that your Heavenly Father is listening for your cry. He is watching over you. And He is going to carry you through!

Just as we pick up our children and carry them, your Heavenly Father is right there, waiting to carry you. As you learn to rely on Him, you can rest in His peace. You can rest in His joy. You can relax in the arms of our Lord Jesus Christ and let Him carry you through all the rough waters of life!

There's Peace in the Throne Room

I'm sure there have been days of turmoil in your life, just as there have been in mine. There have been times when I have gotten down on my knees to pray, and I was so troubled in my spirit. But as I communed with my Heavenly Father, my heart was suddenly flooded with peace!

When we call upon the Lord, He will refresh and restore our souls. He will heal our scars. He will erase the hurtful memories that plague us. And He will heal our emotions so they won't be a hindrance or a stumbling block that can rob us of our peace.

As we come to the throne room of God in prayer, depression will go. Confusion will go and those negative memories will fade away. Our troubled spirits will grow calm and the joy of the Lord will return. Our strength will return. God will restore passion to our hearts—that excitement for the things of God—and the breakthroughs will come. Breakthroughs *will* come—and peace will come—as we call upon the Lord and rest in Him!

CHAPTER 5

Cast Your Cares

"Casting all your care upon him;
for he careth for you."
—1 Peter 5:7

Several years ago, Ken and I experienced what many have called the "empty nest syndrome." Our children were grown and out of the house—either off to college or married—and all of a sudden it was just the two of us!

When our children were growing up, our family had always done things together. Every Friday night at our house was family night. But now it was just Ken and me, and we needed to find something the two of us could do together for fun.

I knew right away that whatever activity we chose would have to involve sports. My husband is extremely talented in the area of sports. In fact, he only has two primary interests in life—sports and preaching.

That put me in a dilemma because I'm not particularly athletic. In fact, sports is my worst talent! If you throw a ball at me, I'm going to try to catch it with my eyes closed. Of course, that doesn't work too well!

So I wondered, *What on earth are we going to do together?*

Now, even though I'm not athletic, I *am* very competitive. So I decided if we were going to develop an interest in sports together, it was going to have to be a sport that Ken didn't know anything about. That way we would at least be on equal ground!

At that time, golf was probably my husband's worst sport involving a ball. I had played putt-putt golf all of my life, so I thought golf might be a good possibility for us. Besides, since the ball would be moving away from me instead of toward me, I wouldn't have to play with my eyes closed!

The only other sports-related activity that Ken hadn't been involved in to any degree was fishing. So I told him, "We can go fishing together as long as you bait my hook and take any fish I catch off the hook for me." He was agreeable to that, so we decided to learn how to fish.

Both of us enjoy eating crappie, so we started fishing for crappie at first. When you fish for crappie, you don't have to cast. You just drop your line into the water and slowly draw it back up. If you don't catch anything, then you drop your line back down and draw it up again.

When we began to fish for crappie, it was wonderful and exciting—at least for a little while. My husband learned how to fillet those crappie, and oh, they tasted good. But they were so small!

Then we decided if we were going to be *real* fishermen, we needed to launch out a little bit further. We knew if we wanted to catch the bigger fish, we were going to have to get a boat. So we went to the boat show, and started shopping for a boat. We finally decided to purchase a bass boat. Of course, if you have a bass boat, you're supposed to catch bass, aren't you?

As soon as we purchased that bass boat, we graduated from fishing for crappie to trolling for sand bass. Those sand bass were good to eat too! But then we saw some plaques with great, big fish mounted on them. And we thought, *Let's go for the big catch—the large mouth bass!*

There we were—we had our bass boat and our fishing rods, and we were ready for some real bass fishing. But all of a sudden we realized if we wanted to catch the big fish, we were going to have to learn how to cast!

Guess what! Casting is not as easy as it sounds. As soon as we started casting our lines into the water, things went wild. We weren't hooking any fish. We were hooking each other's hair! It was not only wild, but it was also dangerous. We were literally taking our lives in our hands!

You see, just because we had a fishing pole in our hands did not mean that we automatically knew how to cast. And if you don't know how to cast, you're not going to catch the prize fish!

So Ken and I started practicing our casting. We would cast out a little at a time and then reel the line back in. Then we would cast out a little farther the next time and reel it back in again. Let me tell you, casting did not come naturally! It took practice. But finally, after much practice, we were able to get those big fish that we so desired to catch!

Casting, Casting, Casting . . .

Did you know that God has some "casting" He wants us to do? The Apostle Peter talks about this in First Peter 5:7.

1 PETER 5:7

7 Casting all your care upon him [God]; for he careth for you.

Why does God want you to cast your cares upon Him? Because "he careth for you!" He's concerned about you. His desire is that you live a life of peace, a life of abundance, and a life of victory. He doesn't want you to be in turmoil all the time. He wants you to cast those burdens on Him—because He loves you so much!

The *Amplified Bible* puts it this way:

1 PETER 5:7 (Amplified)

7 Casting the whole of your care [all your anxieties, all your worries, all your concerns, once and for all] on Him, for He cares for you affectionately and cares about you watchfully.

Notice that this verse says, "Casting all of your anxieties, all of your worries, and all of your concerns *once and for all* upon the Lord." That means after you've cast your cares on the Lord, He doesn't want you to pick them up ever again!

Let's look at a similar scripture in Psalm chapter 55.

PSALM 55:22

22 Cast thy burden upon the Lord, and he shall sustain thee: he shall never suffer the righteous to be moved.

PSALM 55:22 (Amplified)

22 Cast your burden on the Lord [releasing the weight of it] and He will sustain you; He will never allow the [consistently] righteous to be moved (made to slip, fall, or fail).

If we want to experience God's peace—the peace that passes all understanding—we have to cast our cares on the Lord. We have to release the weight of our burdens to Him. What does the last part of that verse say? He will never allow the "consistently righteous"—those who follow wholly after Him—to slip or fall. That verse alone can fill our hearts with peace!

Learning how to cast our cares on the Lord is similar in ways to casting a fishing line. The first time you cast your cares, it may be a total catastrophe! You may feel as if you're getting the fishhooks snagged in your hair. But you have to keep on casting.

When Ken and I started fishing, we only caught the little fish at first. And you may need to start casting the little things on the Lord at first.

For example, if you've been anxious and fretful about everything, pick one of the little things that's been worrying you and cast it on the Lord. After you practice casting the little things, then you can move on to the bigger things. And the more you cast your cares on the Lord, the more you will experience His peace in your heart!

First Corinthians 7:32 (Amplified) says, *"My desire is to have you free from all anxiety and distressing care."* God is saying, "Don't worry! Don't fret! Don't be anxious or lose sleep over anything. You can cast your cares on Me."

Jesus warned us in Luke chapter 12 that being worried and anxious isn't going to accomplish anything at all.

LUKE 12:25–26 (Amplified)

25 And which of you by being overly anxious and troubled with cares can add a cubit to his stature or a moment [unit] of time to his age [the length of his life]?

26 If then you are not able to do such a little thing as that, why are you anxious and troubled with cares about the rest?

If all of our worrying won't add even one inch to our stature or a moment of time to our age, why are we wasting our time worrying about all the other things? But if we will cast our cares and anxieties on the Lord, peace will come, clarity will come, and we will see a complete change in the atmosphere of our lives!

Stay Vigilant

After the Apostle Peter urged us to cast all of our cares upon the Lord, he said something very interesting.

1 PETER 5:8

8 Be sober, be vigilant; because your adversary the devil, as a roaring lion, walketh about, seeking whom he may devour.

1 PETER 5:8 (Amplified)

8 Be well balanced (temperate, sober of mind), be vigilant and cautious at all times; for that enemy of yours, the devil, roams around like a lion roaring [in fierce hunger], seeking someone to seize upon and devour.

Peter is giving us a warning in this verse. He's saying, "When you start casting your cares on the Lord, you'd better watch out for the enemy! The devil will show up to challenge you."

For example, when you declare, "Father, I'm casting the care of my job upon You," the devil will whisper in your ear, "Don't you know that your job is being eliminated? What are you going to do now?" I'll tell you what you're going to do! You're going to declare by faith, "I'm casting my cares on the Lord!"

When you cast the care of your finances on the Lord, the devil will threaten you, saying, "You don't have enough money to pay your bills! What are you going to do now?" That's when you can declare by faith, "I'm casting my cares on the Lord. My God will supply all of my needs, according to His riches in glory by Christ Jesus (Phil. 4:19)."

Or if you begin to cast the care of your health on the Lord, all of a sudden the devil will yell in your ear, "Don't you know you're not healed? Your body is racked with pain." But you can just declare to him, "The Word of God says that with the stripes of Jesus, I am healed (1 Pet. 2:24). I'm casting my cares on the Lord!"

There have been times in my life when the burdens and concerns were threatening to overwhelm me. I would try desperately not to worry. I knew I was supposed to cast my cares on the Lord, and I always endeavored to do that. But the devil would keep bringing those troublesome thoughts back to my mind.

Finally, the Lord said to me, "These are mere distractions to keep you from doing what I have called you to do." Mere distractions!

Don't let the devil distract you from your calling! Don't let him distract you from your destiny! We all have a destiny to fulfill and we must not allow the devil to distract us with worry, fear, or anxiety.

Not only will worry harm us mentally and spiritually, but it can harm us physically too. Worry can make us sick. And worry is a sin! There are so many verses in the Bible where the Lord Himself told us not to worry (Matt. 6:25, 31, 34; Luke 12:22, 29).

Of course, Satan purposely creates things for us to worry about. He loves to get us so entangled in worries, stress, and the cares of life that we can no longer concentrate on our Father's business.

But if we're going to have peace in our hearts and rise to the level that God has destined for us, we're going to have to cast all of our cares and worries on Him. We must declare, "Once and for all I'm casting these things on the Lord," and we must never allow them into our thought life again!

Start Casting!

If you have a care, if you have a concern that's been dogging you on the inside, it's time to cast that over on the Lord! If you've been distraught or discouraged about anything at all or if you're struggling with worry and fear, I encourage you to cast those burdens on the Lord right now.

When we cast our cares on the Lord, it soothes our troubled minds. It brings so much peace to our hearts. And it moves us into a position where God can speak to us more clearly. It keeps our relationship with our Heavenly Father fresh and new every day!

Where there has been discouragement, there will be joy. Where there has been frustration, there will be

49

tranquility. And where there has been turmoil, we can rest in God's peace.

When the worries and circumstances of life arise, we're going to say, "I'm casting, I'm casting!" As we cast our cares on the Lord, He's going to bring us through all the trials and all the hard places—right through them! And we're going to come out on the other side of those problems rejoicing, with the peace of God flooding our hearts!

CHAPTER 6

Run to the Word!

*"Great peace have they
which love thy law."*
—Psalm 119:165

There's nothing like the Word of God that can keep our minds and hearts in peace. During the troubled times—when worry and depression try to overtake us—we can always run to God's Word. His Word is our safety in the midst of harm!

Reading God's Word and meditating on the Word are so important if we are going to keep our minds in peace. Why? Because the Word *is* our peace. And true peace can only come through the Word of God.

There are all kinds of scriptures in the Bible which focus on peace. I encourage you to find those scriptures, meditate on them, and they will give you peace. (I will share some of my favorite peace scriptures with you at the end of this book.)

One of the most important scriptures that I was taught all of my life is Matthew 6:33—*"But seek ye first*

51

*the kingdom of God, and his righteousness; and all
these things shall be added unto you."*

If you don't have peace, if you're not having all of
these other "things" added to you, I encourage you to
check up on what you're seeking. Are you seeking the
things of this world—social position, fame, fortune,
worldly success? Or are you seeking God's Word? Are
you seeking the Lord, or is He taking a backseat in
your life?

If we want to put God first, we must surround ourselves with a godly environment. Of course, we live in a
busy world, and we don't always have a lot of time to
spend meditating on God's Word. But do you know what
I try to do on a daily basis? Regardless of where I am, I
surround myself with some form of the Word.

When I am at home, there is Christian music playing
24 hours a day—songs that talk about the Word of God,
the blood of Jesus, the Cross, and His peace, wonderful
peace! I want my home to be filled with God's Word.
When I walk into that house, I want it to be permeated
with the anointing of the Holy Spirit.

As soon as I wake up in the morning, the first thing
I want to hear is good, Christian music. If I awaken in
the middle of the night and my mind has been giving me
trouble—perhaps I've had a night of waking up—I
want to hear a song that brings peace to my heart.

We need to surround ourselves with God's Word—
and not just in our homes. The minute I get into my car,

I turn on one of my five favorite CDs, and I play those songs over and over again. If my husband and I are traveling, we play good Christian music in our hotel room day and night.

That's how I keep my mind peaceful. That's how I rest in the Lord. I meditate on my Heavenly Father constantly. I meditate on His Word constantly. I always keep myself surrounded with the promises of God!

Don't Neglect the Word

It's more important today than ever before that we build a strong foundation in God's Word and make His Word a daily part of our lives. Sometimes our schedules are so busy that we think we don't have time to read and meditate on the Word. But we always seem to have time to do the things we *want* to do!

For example, we have time to read the newspaper. We have time to watch our favorite programs on television. We can always find time to do all the other things that are important to us. But are we making time to do the things that will cause us to walk in God's peace? Are we learning to be grounded in the Word and not moved by what we see with our natural eyes? Are we learning to trust in the Lord and cast our cares on Him? Those are the things that will cause peace to rule in our hearts.

If you truly want to make God's Word a daily part of your life, I encourage you to consider fasting something that may be keeping you from spending time in the

53

Word. Sometimes we don't realize how much a certain activity is consuming our time until we fast some of it.

Brother Hagin always encouraged people to live a fasted life. What did he mean by that? Every day of your life, fast something.

We usually think of fasting as merely food, but fasting doesn't always mean food. Did you know that we can fast other things? For example, we can fast some of our time on the computer. We can fast some of the time we spend watching television. Or we can fast text messaging. Oh, dear Lord! This generation doesn't even like to have a conversation unless it's through e-mails or text messages!

What does fasting accomplish? It helps us crucify the flesh—keep our flesh under control (Gal. 5:24). If we want to have peace, we sometimes need to bring our flesh into subjection (1 Cor. 9:27).

Of course, something that is a time consumer for me may not be a time consumer for you. For example, I receive numerous shopping magazines in the mail and looking through them used to consume a lot of my time.

At first, they were actually saving me time because I was ordering everything online instead of going shopping. I thought, *This is a real time saver. I'm going to have so much time to do other things.* But that's the way the enemy gets us hooked on things. He comes to us so subtly!

At one point, I became so engrossed in looking through those shopping magazines that I was spending more time doing that than I was seeking the Lord. But as the Word tells us, we need to "seek the Lord while He may be found" (Isa. 55:6).

What did I do to break loose from that time-consuming habit? For a certain period of time, I stopped looking through any of those shopping magazines. I simply put them aside. Later, I was able to enjoy looking through a few of them and throw the rest away.

The same thing will be true for you if you try fasting something that's consuming too much of your time. You'll find that when you go back to it, it doesn't consume as much of your time as it used to. And you will be amazed at how much time you actually have to meditate on the Word!

Of course, looking through magazines is not a sin. Watching television or spending time on the computer is not a sin. But sometimes we need to break loose from those bondages.

The Apostle Paul said in Hebrews 12:1, *"let us lay aside every weight . . . which doth so easily beset us."* In these last days, we need to be about the Father's business. In order to do that, we must set aside the weights that hinder us. We must seek first the kingdom of God and give His Word first place.

If we're not careful, we will find ourselves living a life of powerlessness, a life without peace, simply because we've neglected the very thing that will give us God's power and His peace—the Word of God.

If we let ourselves be consumed with all the natural things of life, that's what will come out when the tests and trials come. We will wring our hands and cry out to the Lord, "What are we going to do now?"

But if we set aside the time to fill our minds and hearts with the Word, when the crisis times come, we can boldly declare that we're not going under—we're going over! And we can have peace—not turmoil, not discouragement, not worry and distress—in the middle of any storm or struggle!

Are You Meeting the Conditions of God's Word?

There are so many verses in the Bible that talk about the importance of God's Word. Let's read several of those verses from the Book of Deuteronomy.

DEUTERONOMY 11:18–24

18 Therefore shall ye lay up these my words in your heart and in your soul, and bind them for a sign upon your hand, that they may be as frontlets between your eyes.

19 And ye shall teach them your children, speaking of them when thou sittest in thine house, and when thou walkest by the way, when thou liest down, and when thou risest up.

20 And thou shalt write them upon the door posts of thine house, and upon thy gates:

21 That your days may be multiplied, and the days of your children, in the land which the Lord sware unto

your fathers to give them, as the days of heaven upon the earth.

22 For if ye shall diligently keep all these commandments which I command you, to do them, to love the Lord your God, to walk in all his ways, and to cleave unto him;

23 Then will the Lord drive out all these nations from before you, and ye shall possess greater nations and mightier than yourselves.

24 Every place whereon the soles of your feet shall tread shall be yours.

What do these verses say God is going to do if we will diligently keep His commandments, His Word? First of all, He's going to drive the enemies out of our lives— enemies of sickness, enemies of financial lack, enemies of discouragement, depression, and fear. These are the things that rob us of our peace! Then it goes on to say, "Every place where the soles of your feet shall tread shall be yours."

Sometimes we wonder why we're not receiving the promises of God. We wonder why we're being battered by one crisis after the other, why we have so little victory, and why we have no peace. We wonder why our world seems to be crumbling around us.

Yes, we're claiming the promises of God. We're confessing the Word. But our confession is powerless. Why? Because we're not doing what these verses from the Book of Deuteronomy tell us to do. We're not obeying the rest of God's Word.

With every promise of God there are conditions. The Lord said if we would hide His Word in our hearts and continually do what it tells us to do, *then* every place where the soles of our feet shall tread shall be ours. Instead of grabbing hold of what is ours to possess, we've become disappointed and disillusioned. We've decided, *This faith stuff doesn't work!*

Yes, it does work! But it won't work for us, personally, if we're not meeting the conditions in God's Word!

In John 15:7, Jesus gives us some instructions to help us meet the conditions of His Word.

JOHN 15:7

7 If ye abide in me, and my words abide in you, ye shall ask what ye will, and it shall be done unto you.

If we abide in Him and His Words abide in us! How do we abide in the Lord? We abide in Him by reading His Word, communing with Him in prayer, and keeping our hearts and minds focused on Him.

Notice what God says we will have if we abide in Him—"Whatsoever things we ask." That means we're going to receive whatever we need from Him, and that includes His peace! But the most important qualification for receiving from God is abiding in Him—giving Him first place. Everything else should come after the Lord!

Walking Over Circumstances

Sometimes people wonder, *Why should I spend so much time meditating on God's Word?* I'll tell you why!

When the pressure times come, when discouragement is clouding your mind, those verses that you've hidden in your heart will start coming out of your mouth. And God's Word will give you peace in the middle of every storm!

Do you realize that when Peter stepped out on the water to walk toward Jesus, he wouldn't have started sinking if he had kept his eyes on the Savior? But what did he do? He let the circumstances around him—the wind rising and the storm brewing—cause fear to grip his heart. When he began to fear, he lost his peace. And when he lost his peace, he started to sink (Matt. 14:28–30).

The same thing is true in your life. When you keep your eyes focused on the Word of God, His Word will help you walk on top of the circumstances. But if you begin to focus on your problems and troubles, you're going to sink.

Of course, the waters of your life won't always be smooth. There may be stumbling blocks in your path. The winds may be howling and the waves may be crashing all around you. But don't let the enemy distract you with those things. He's just trying to keep you from your ultimate course in life!

Yes, you recognize that the circumstances are there. But you also recognize that God is on your side. And if God is for you, who can be against you (Rom. 8:31)? You can walk over the top of those circumstances because God is on your side!

Don't let anything—any person, any circumstance, or even the devil himself—keep you from receiving what God has for you. And don't let Satan keep you from walking in God's peace!

If you're facing problems and heartaches right now—if you're struggling and cannot seem to find any peace—remember that your Heavenly Father is watching over you. Look to Him! Reach out to Him. Grab hold of His hand. He will lead you safely to the other side of that problem or struggle!

Don't be moved by what you see with your natural eyes. Be moved by God's Word! Take the medicine of God's Word (Prov. 4:22). I guarantee that it will heal your mind. It will heal your body. It will heal your emotions. It will heal your home. It will bring your children back to the Lord. And there will be no harmful side effects—just God's perfect peace flooding over your heart!

Peace Scriptures

Meditate on these scriptures and allow the Word of God to provide you with the peace you need for every one of life's situations.

The Twenty-Third Psalm

PSALM 23:1–6

1   The Lord is my shepherd; I shall not want.

2   He maketh me to lie down in green pastures: he leadeth me beside the still waters.

3   He restoreth my soul: he leadeth me in the paths of righteousness for his name's sake.

4   Yea, though I walk through the valley of the shadow of death, I will fear no evil: for thou art with me; thy rod and thy staff they comfort me.

5   Thou preparest a table before me in the presence of mine enemies: thou anointest my head with oil; my cup runneth over.

6   Surely goodness and mercy shall follow me all the days of my life: and I will dwell in the house of the Lord for ever.

PSALM 23:1–6 (Amplified)

1 The Lord is my Shepherd [to feed, guide, and shield me], I shall not lack.

2 He makes me lie down in [fresh, tender] green pastures; He leads me beside the still and restful waters.

3 He refreshes and restores my life (my self); He leads me in the paths of righteousness [uprightness and right standing with Him—not for my earning it, but] for His name's sake.

4 Yes, though I walk through the [deep, sunless] valley of the shadow of death, I will fear or dread no evil, for You are with me; Your rod [to protect] and Your staff [to guide], they comfort me.

5 You prepare a table before me in the presence of my enemies. You anoint my head with oil; my [brimming] cup runs over.

6 Surely or only goodness, mercy, and unfailing love shall follow me all the days of my life, and through the length of my days the house of the Lord [and His presence] shall be my dwelling place.

Peaceful Sleep and Rest

MATTHEW 11:28–29 (Amplified)

28 Come to Me, all you who labor and are heavy-laden and overburdened, and I will cause you to rest. [I will ease and relieve and refresh your souls.]

29 Take My yoke upon you and learn of Me, for I am gentle (meek) and humble (lowly) in heart, and you will find rest (relief and ease and refreshment and recreation and blessed quiet) for your souls.

HEBREWS 4:3 (Amplified)

3 For we who have believed (adhered to and trusted in and relied on God) do enter that rest.

PSALM 16:9

9 Therefore my heart is glad, and my glory rejoiceth: my flesh also shall rest in hope.

JOB 11:18

18 And thou shalt be secure, because there is hope; yea, thou shalt dig about thee, and thou shalt take thy rest in safety.

EXODUS 33:14

14 And he said, My presence shall go with thee, and I will give thee rest.

1 KINGS 8:56 (Amplified)

56 Blessed be the Lord, Who has given rest to His people Israel, according to all that He promised. Not one word has failed of all His good promise which He promised through Moses His servant.

1 CHRONICLES 22:18 (Amplified)

18 Is not the Lord your God with you? And has He not given you peace on every side?

1 CHRONICLES 23:25 (Amplified)

25 For David said, The Lord, the God of Israel has given peace and rest to His people, and He dwells in Jerusalem forever.

PSALM 4:8 (Amplified)

8 In peace I will both lie down and sleep, for You, Lord, alone make me dwell in safety and confident trust.

PROVERBS 3:24 (Amplified)

24 When you lie down, you shall not be afraid; yes, you shall lie down, and your sleep shall be sweet.

ISAIAH 32:18 (Amplified)

18 My people shall dwell in a peaceable habitation, in safe dwellings, and in quiet resting-places.

ISAIAH 14:3

3 And it shall come to pass in the day that the Lord shall give thee rest from thy sorrow.

PSALM 37:7

7 Rest in the Lord, and wait patiently for him: fret not thyself because of him who prospereth in his way.

PROVERBS 1:33 (Amplified)

33 But whoso hearkens to me [Wisdom] shall dwell securely and in confident trust and shall be quiet, without fear or dread of evil.

2 THESSALONIANS 3:16

16 Now the Lord of peace himself give you peace always by all means. The Lord be with you all.

Relationships of Peace

PROVERBS 16:7 (Amplified)

7 When a man's ways please the Lord, He makes even his enemies to be at peace with him.

PSALM 122:7

7 Peace be within thy walls, and prosperity within thy palaces.

PSALM 55:18 (NASB)

18 He will redeem my soul in peace from the battle which is against me.

PSALM 147:14 (Message)

14 He keeps the peace at your borders, he puts the best bread on your tables.

PSALM 34:14

14 Depart from evil, and do good; seek peace, and pursue it.

ISAIAH 49:25 (Amplified)

25 I will give safety to your children and ease them.

ISAIAH 54:13 (Amplified)

13 And all your . . . children shall be disciples [taught by the Lord and obedient to His will], and great shall be the peace and undisturbed composure of your children.

MATTHEW 5:9

9 Blessed are the peacemakers: for they shall be called the children of God.

ISAIAH 26:12 (Amplified)

12 Lord, You will ordain peace (God's favor and blessings, both temporal and spiritual) for us.

ISAIAH 32:18 (Message)

18 My people will live in a peaceful neighborhood—in safe houses, in quiet gardens.

ZECHARIAH 8:16 (Amplified)

16 These are the things that you shall do: speak every man the truth with his neighbor; render the truth and pronounce the judgment or verdict that makes for peace in [the courts at] your gates.

ISAIAH 52:7 (Amplified)

7 How beautiful upon the mountains are the feet of him who brings good tidings, who publishes peace, who brings good tidings of good, who publishes salvation, who says to Zion, Your God reigns!

HEBREWS 12:14 (Amplified)

14 Strive to live in peace with everybody and pursue that consecration and holiness without which no one will [ever] see the Lord.

ROMANS 14:19

19 Let us therefore follow after the things which make for peace, and things wherewith one may edify another.

EPHESIANS 2:14

14 For he is our peace, who hath made both one, and hath broken down the middle wall of partition between us.

Peace for Troubling Thoughts

JEREMIAH 29:11

11 For I know the thoughts that I think toward you, saith the Lord, thoughts of peace, and not of evil, to give you an expected end.

1 CORINTHIANS 14:33

33 For God is not the author of confusion, but of peace.

PSALM 94:19 (Amplified)

19 In the multitude of my [anxious] thoughts within me, Your comforts cheer and delight my soul!

ISAIAH 26:3 (MKJV)

3 You will keep him in perfect peace, whose mind is stayed on You; because he trusts in You.

ISAIAH 26:3 (Message)

3 People with their minds set on you, you keep completely whole, Steady on their feet, because they keep at it and don't quit.

ROMANS 5:1

1 Therefore being justified by faith, we have peace with God through our Lord Jesus Christ.

ROMANS 8:6

6 For to be carnally minded is death; but to be spiritually minded is life and peace.

PSALM 29:11

11 The Lord will bless his people with peace.

MATTHEW 6:31–34 (Amplified)

31 Therefore do not worry and be anxious, saying, What are we going to have to eat? or, What are we going to have to drink? or, What are we going to have to wear?

32 For the Gentiles (heathen) wish for and crave and diligently seek all these things, and your heavenly Father knows well that you need them all.

33 But seek (aim at and strive after) first of all His kingdom and His righteousness (His way of doing and

being right), and then all these things taken together will be given you besides.

34 So do not worry or be anxious about tomorrow, for tomorrow will have worries and anxieties of its own.

PHILIPPIANS 4:7 (MKJV)

7 And the peace of God which passes all understanding shall keep your hearts and minds through Christ Jesus.

Jesus Is Our Peace

ISAIAH 9:6

6 For unto us a child is born, unto us a son is given: and the government shall be upon his shoulder: and his name shall be called Wonderful, Counsellor, The mighty God, The everlasting Father, The Prince of Peace.

ISAIAH 53:5

5 But he was wounded for our transgressions, he was bruised for our iniquities: the chastisement of our peace was upon him; and with his stripes we are healed.

LUKE 2:14

14 Glory to God in the highest, and on earth peace, good will toward men.

JOHN 14:23, 25–27 (Amplified)

23 Jesus answered, If a person [really] loves Me, he will keep My word. . . .

25 I have told you these things while I am still with you.

26 But the Comforter (Counselor, Helper, Intercessor, Advocate, Strengthener, Standby), the Holy Spirit, Whom the Father will send in My name [in My place, to represent Me and act on My behalf], He will teach you all things. And He will cause you to recall (will remind you of, bring to your remembrance) everything I have told you.

27 Peace I leave with you; My [own] peace I now give and bequeath to you. Not as the world gives do I give to you. Do not let your hearts be troubled, neither let them be afraid. [Stop allowing yourselves to be agitated and disturbed; and do not permit yourselves to be fearful and intimidated and cowardly and unsettled.]

LUKE 24:36 (Amplified)

36 Now while they were talking about this, Jesus Himself took His stand among them and said to them, Peace (freedom from all the distresses that are experienced as the result of sin) be to you!

JOHN 16:33 (MKJV)

33 I have spoken these things to you so that you might have peace in Me. In the world you shall have tribulation, but be of good cheer. I have overcome the world.

Lifestyles of Peace

1 PETER 3:10–11 (Amplified)

10 For let him who wants to enjoy life and see good days . . . keep his tongue free from evil and his lips from guile (treachery, deceit).

11 Let him turn away from wickedness and shun it, and let him do right. Let him search for peace (harmony; undisturbedness from fears, agitating passions, and moral conflicts) and seek it eagerly. [Do not merely desire peaceful relations with God, with your fellow-men, and with yourself, but pursue, go after them!]

JAMES 3:18

18 And the fruit of righteousness is sown in peace of them that make peace.

PSALM 37:11

11 But the meek shall inherit the earth; and shall delight themselves in the abundance of peace.

1 TIMOTHY 2:1–3

1 I exhort therefore, that, first of all, supplications, prayers, intercessions, and giving of thanks, be made for all men;

2 For kings, and for all that are in authority; that we may lead a quiet and peaceable life in all godliness and honesty.

3 For this is good and acceptable in the sight of God our Saviour.

ISAIAH 32:17

17 And the work of righteousness shall be peace; and the effect of righteousness quietness and assurance for ever.

PHILIPPIANS 4:9

9 Those things, which ye have both learned, and received, and heard, and seen in me, do: and the God of peace shall be with you.

Comfort

PSALM 119:50 (Amplified)

50 This is my comfort and consolation in my affliction: that Your word has revived me and given me life.

MATTHEW 5:4

4 Blessed are they that mourn: for they shall be comforted.

2 CORINTHIANS 1:3–4 (Amplified)

3 Blessed be the God and Father of our Lord Jesus Christ, the Father of sympathy (pity and mercy) and the God [Who is the Source] of every comfort (consolation and encouragement),

4 Who comforts (consoles and encourages) us in every trouble (calamity and affliction), so that we may also be able to comfort (console and encourage) those who are in any kind of trouble or distress, with the comfort (consolation and encouragement) with which we ourselves are comforted (consoled and encouraged) by God.

JOHN 14:16–18 (Amplified)

16 And I will ask the Father, and He will give you another Comforter (Counselor, Helper, Intercessor, Advocate, Strengthener, and Standby), that He may remain with you forever—

17 The Spirit of Truth, Whom the world cannot receive (welcome, take to its heart), because it does not see Him or know and recognize Him. But you know and recognize Him, for He lives with you [constantly] and will be in you.

18 I will not leave you as orphans [comfortless, desolate, bereaved, forlorn, helpless]; I will come [back] to you.

2 CORINTHIANS 13:11 (Amplified)

11 Finally, brethren, farewell (rejoice)! Be strengthened (perfected, completed, made what you ought to be); be encouraged and consoled and comforted; be of the same [agreeable] mind one with another; live in peace, and [then] the God of love [Who is the Source of affection, goodwill, love, and benevolence toward men] and the Author and Promoter of peace will be with you.

Closing Thoughts From God's Word

ROMANS 14:17

17 For the kingdom of God is not meat and drink; but righteousness, and peace, and joy in the Holy Ghost.

1 CORINTHIANS 7:15 (Amplified)

15 But God has called us to peace.

PSALM 119:165

165 Great peace have they which love thy law.

NUMBERS 6:24–26 (Amplified)

24 The Lord bless you and watch, guard, and keep you;

25 The Lord make His face to shine upon and enlighten you and be gracious (kind, merciful, and giving favor) to you;

26 The Lord lift up His [approving] countenance upon you and give you peace (tranquility of heart and life continually).

Notes

Chapter 1

1. Merriam-Webster's Collegiate Dictionary, 11th ed. (Springfield, MA: Merriam-Webster, Inc., 2003), 911.

2. *Brown, Driver, Briggs, Gesenius Lexicon*, "Shalowm," http://www.biblestudytools.com/search/?q=peace&s=References&rc=LEX&rc2=LEX+HEB.

3. W.C. Martin, 1921. Music by Charles H. Gabriel. "My Father Watches Over Me." Public Domain.

Chapter 3

1. David Ingles, "My Confidence Is Great (In the Lord)." Copyright © 1991 David Ingles Music. Used with permission. www.diministries.org.

2. Merriam-Webster's Collegiate Dictionary, 11th ed. (Springfield, MA: Merriam-Webster, Inc., 2003), 1344.

3. Andraé Crouch. "Through It All." Copyright © 1971. Renewed 1999 by Manna Music, Inc., All rights reserved. Used with permission. (ASCAP)

4. Robert W. Sutton "To Illustrate . . ." Leadership Journal Fall (October 1988), http://www.christianitytoday.com/le/1988/fall/88l4044.html?start=3

5. Louisa M.R. Stead, 1882. "'Tis So Sweet to Trust in Jesus." Public Domain.

Why should you consider attending

Rhema
Bible Training Center?